PATRICK
Patron Saint of Ireland

PATRICK

Patron Saint of Ireland

by Tomie dePaola

Holiday House / New York

To my Irish mother,
Flossie Downey dePaola

TdeP

Special thanks to my studio
assistant, Raphael Noz,
for his generous help

TdeP

Copyright © 1992 by Tomie dePaola

Printed in Mexico

All rights reserved

Library of Congress Cataloging-in-Publication Data
De Paola, Tomie.
Patrick : patron saint of Ireland / by Tomie dePaola.
p.   cm.
Summary: Relates the life and legends of Patrick,
the patron saint of Ireland.
ISBN 0-8234-0924-4
1. Patrick, Saint, 373?–463?—Juvenile literature.
.2. Christian saints—Ireland—Biography—Juvenile
literature.
[1. Patrick, Saint, 373?–463? 2. Saints.] I. Title.
BR1720.P26D46   1992   91-19417   CIP   AC
270.2′092—dc20
[B]
ISBN 0-8234-1077-3 (pbk)

Many years ago, during the time of the Christian Roman Empire, there lived a boy named Patrick. He lived with his noble family in Britain, near the Irish sea.

One night, fierce Irishmen from the island across the water came in their boats and raided the farms on the British mainland.

They captured many people—Patrick among them. They took him
back to Ireland and sold him as a slave to a man named Miliucc.

"Now that I own you," said Miliucc, "I will take you to Mount Slemish, where you shall watch my sheep."

For six years, in the strange and pagan land, Patrick, who was used to warm clothes, good food, and a nice house, was a shepherd, and he was very lonely. All he could do was pray to God over and over and over again—a hundred times during the day, a hundred times during the night. And he felt the love of God in his heart.

Patrick's prayers did not go unanswered. During his sleep, a voice came to him: "It is a good thing that you fast and pray, for soon you will go to your own country. See, your ship is ready."

The ship was more than two hundred miles away, but that didn't stop Patrick. Believing in the strength of God, Patrick went on his way, fearing nothing.

Now, the ship was filled with hunting hounds that were being taken to France to be sold to rich people. When the hounds saw Patrick, they stopped barking and began to wag their tails.

Patrick offered to pay for his passage, but the captain worried that he might be an escaped slave and said, ''I cannot take you with us. Get off my ship.''

So Patrick left. He began to pray that the captain would change his mind. The hounds started to howl.

"Those hounds were fine when that fellow was here," said one of the men. "But now they're making so much noise, they'll raise the dead."

"Run and get him," said the captain, "or else we will have no peace on our journey."

Patrick's prayers were answered. He was allowed to board the ship, and it set sail.

After three days, the ship landed. The countryside was deserted because there had been a war. For twenty-eight days, the men and the hounds traveled through the desolate land, finally overcome with hunger.

"Tell me, Christian," the captain said. "You say that your God is great and all-powerful. Why don't you pray for us, then? Can't you see how hungry we are?"

"Nothing is impossible for my God," Patrick answered. "This day, He will send food to us."

Suddenly, a herd of pigs appeared on the road in front of them, oinking and squealing. The men caught and killed them. For two days, everyone, including the dogs, had plenty to eat. And they did not go hungry again.

Soon, Patrick left the little group and traveled alone for two years. When he finally arrived back home in Britain, his family rejoiced and begged him never to leave them again.

Once more, Patrick had a dream. This time, a man named Victoricus appeared to him. Victoricus had come from Ireland with an armload of letters. He gave one of them to Patrick. It read, "The voice of the Irish." Then Patrick heard voices calling from the woods: "Come and walk among us again."

Patrick woke up. He wasn't sure what the dream meant. A few nights later, Patrick heard more voices calling to him, and then he knew what he must do.

He must return to Ireland and take the people the good news of God.

Although it was hard to part with his family, Patrick left home to study and become a missionary. Finally, he was ready to sail for Ireland and take the word of God to the Irish people. He sold his worldly goods, bought all he needed for his work, and hired a boat.

A huge crowd went along to help him: priests, bakers, chariot drivers—all kinds of people. Patrick was now a bishop, and the work that God had planned for him was about to begin.

Shortly after the ship landed in Ireland, Patrick met a chieftain who was a good and kind man. This chieftain's name was Dichu, and he listened to Patrick talk of his love of God. He believed everything that Patrick told him and asked Patrick to baptize him into the new faith. Dichu gave Patrick the barn that became the first church in Ireland.

But not everything that happened to Patrick was so easy.

Patrick's chariot driver, Odran, overheard that a king planned to kill Patrick. Odran wanted to protect his master.

''Bishop Patrick,'' he said. ''Would you be so kind as to drive the chariot today? I am very tired.''

So Patrick agreed. As they were driving, the king threw his spear and killed Odran, thinking he was the bishop. Patrick escaped, but he was sad knowing that his friend Odran had given up his life to protect him.

Patrick faced many other dangers, too. In fact, he came close to losing his life twelve times. But that didn't stop him. Through the years, he traveled many, many miles and baptized thousands of people.

On March 17, 461, Patrick died. Patrick's love of God had been so great that shortly after his death, churches were built all over the land, and Patrick was made a saint. Young men and women became monks and priests and nuns. They served the people of Ireland in the churches, monasteries, and schools. They traveled to other lands, preaching the love of God, just as Patrick had done when he came to the Emerald Isle. And even to this day, the Irish love their patron saint, Patrick.

There are many legends about Saint Patrick. Here are a few of them.

Saint Patrick and the Snakes

Some people say there are no snakes in Ireland because Saint Patrick drove them out, just as he had driven out sin. Patrick got rid of the snakes by beating a drum hard and fast. The snakes couldn't stand the noise, so they slithered into the sea.

Saint Patrick and the Lost Horses

One dark night, Patrick's chariot driver lost his horses. It was so dark that he couldn't even look for them. Patrick raised his hand, and each of his five fingers lit up. In the light, the chariot driver was able to find his lost horses.

Saint Patrick and the Evil Coroticus

Coroticus was a cruel ruler. He persecuted Christians. Patrick sent him a letter, asking him to stop, but Coroticus paid no attention to it. When Patrick heard this, he prayed to God to punish the evil ruler. Right in front of all of Coroticus's followers, God changed Coroticus into a fox. The fox ran off and was never seen again.

Saint Patrick and the Altar Stone

Saint Patrick was returning to Ireland from a visit to Rome. He had a large altar stone with him. The captain of the ship that was to take Patrick on the last leg of the journey refused to take the stone on board. "There is no room," he said, "and besides, that stone is too heavy." Patrick got angry at the captain. He picked up the stone and threw it behind the boat. The stone floated and Patrick sat on it, riding the stone all the way home in the wake of the ship.

Saint Patrick and the Shamrock

When Saint Patrick was preaching about the Holy Trinity, the people could not understand that there was one God in three Divine Persons: the Father, the Son, and the Holy Spirit. Patrick looked down, and growing at his feet was a shamrock. He picked it and held it up, showing that there was one stem, but three leaves. The people understood the Holy Trinity at once.

I first became aware of St. Patrick, the great patron saint of the Irish, when I was a young child. My older brother Joe and I had spent Saturday night with my Irish grandparents, Tom and Alice Downey, in Wallingford, Connecticut. Because my grandfather opened his grocery store for several hours on Sunday mornings for the customers who had ''forgotten things,'' my brother and I went with him to ''first mass'' at Holy Trinity Church. We walked into the dark church and sat up front in my grandfather's regular pew. On the side altar in front of us was a very colorful statue of a saint holding a staff in one hand, a shamrock in the other. At his feet, squirming and squiggling into the plaster water, were green snakes.

''That's Saint Patrick,'' my grandfather said. ''He's Irish, just like us.''

I immediately forgot that I was half-Italian. Every year after that, I celebrated St. Patrick's Day with gusto, decorating my room with shamrocks. My brother took Patrick for his confirmation name. My Italian father celebrated, too, claiming Patrick was from Italy.

My Irish mother, Flossie Downey dePaola, has been after me for years to remember the Irish patron saint with a book. Here it is.

And as the Irish shout on March 17, ''Erin go bragh!'' (''Ireland forever!'')

TdeP
August 15, 1991